INDEX

Ladybird books recommended for further reading on subjects mentioned in this book:

Series 601

> Great Inventions
> Exploring Space
> The Story of Radio
> The Story of Nuclear Power
> The Story of Medicine

Series 708

> Madame Curie
> Michael Faraday

Series 536

> The Night Sky
> Your Body

Series 654

> How it works—The Camera
> How it works—Television
> How it works—The Telescope and Microscope
> How it works—The Computer

Series 621

> Magnets, Bulbs and Batteries
> Light, Mirrors and Lenses
> Air, Wind and Flight
> Levers, Pulleys and Engines

The publishers wish to acknowledge the advice and assistance of A. P. Sanday, M.A., Science Adviser, Warwickshire, L.E.A., when preparing this book.

Book 2

The story of
Science

by EDMUND HUNTER
with illustrations
by B. H. ROBINSON

Ladybird Books Ltd Loughborough

The work of Galileo

Galileo is perhaps best known for his work on the telescope; in fact he did more than any other man to lay firm foundations for the study of physical science. His most important and original work was the establishment of the science of dynamics (or force in motion), by experiment and by studying mathematically the movement of objects.

He disproved many of the old theories, including the teaching that if a heavy iron ball were dropped from a height it would fall more quickly than a light one. There is a story that he proved his point by dropping two iron balls from the top of the Leaning Tower of Pisa. One weighed ten pounds (4.5kg), the other one pound (0.45kg); both reached the ground at the same time.

Another story concerns his discovery of the principle of the pendulum while watching a swinging lamp hanging from the roof of the cathedral at Pisa. He observed that each swing of the lamp took the same time, whether the length of the swing was long or short. Many years later, just before he died, he applied this principle to the working of a clock.

From his observations on moving objects, Galileo concluded that once anything started to move it would continue to do so until something acted to stop it. He used this 'principle of inertia' to explain why the planets need no force to keep them moving.

In 1638 his book 'Discourses and Mathematical Demonstrations Concerning Two New Sciences' was published. It was printed in Leyden, Holland, for fear of causing further trouble for him in his own country.

Opposite (above) Galileo and the movement of a pendulum clock.
(below) The cathedral lamp gives Galileo an idea.

0 7214 0354 9

Isaac Newton

Isaac Newton (1642–1727) was a brilliant mathematician, astronomer and philosopher, and is considered to have been one of the world's greatest men of science. He, and others, finally showed that the kind of force which causes an apple to fall to the ground is the same as that which keeps the moon orbiting the earth, and the planets orbiting the sun – the force called gravity.

He carried on the work of Galileo, and his laws of motion were the basis on which astronomers and physicists have researched for nearly three hundred years. These laws are very much in evidence today in this age of rocketry and space travel. In 1687 he published his great book 'The Mathematical Principles of Natural Philosophy', better known as the 'Principia'.

Later scientists owed much to Edmund Halley, Newton's friend; without his persuasion the book would probably never have been written or published. Halley applied Newton's principles to working out the paths of the comets. He rightly predicted that a comet which appeared in 1682 would reappear at the end of 1758. This reappearance of the comet convinced the scientific world that Newton's ideas and calculations were correct. Halley's Comet, as it is called, was last seen in 1910 and is due to be seen again in 1986. It is the same comet pictured in the Bayeux Tapestry, and at that time it was believed that its appearance foretold disaster.

Newton's diagram shows the differing tracks of a projectile if launched at different speeds from a great height above the Earth. At the right speed and height it would orbit the Earth as do our present day satellites.

STELLA

Halley's Comet is pictured on the Bayeux Tapestry.
(Left) Halley and (right) an impression of the comet

Mathematics and magnetism

In the 17th century there was remarkable progress in the development of mathematics. Newton's theory of motion was explained by him in mathematical terms and those who began to apply it were all mathematicians. They used a new form of mathematics that solved problems by algebra as well as by geometry. Algebra had been known to the Arabs many centuries before, but its use was now extended with astonishing skill. Newton also developed a mathematical system which is known today as calculus. This was helpful in the working out of problems concerned with constantly changing situations such as the movement of planets and other bodies.

Mathematical advances at that time did much to encourage further experiment and progress in other forms of science such as astronomy, force and motion, and the flight of projectiles.

In 1600, William Gilbert, a physician of Queen Elizabeth I, published a book called 'De Magneta' (About the Magnet). Magnetic compasses made of lodestone had been used in ships for more than five hundred years but nobody had previously worked out a theory about magnetism. Gilbert put forward the idea that the Earth is itself a huge magnet. He also tried to find the reason a magnet does not point towards the true north. He designed instruments to help him in his work and, wherever possible, checked his theories by experiment.

The reason for the Earth's magnetism is still being investigated.

N   S N   S   N   S   S   N

Gilbert discovered the basic law of magnetism: unlike poles attract - like poles repel

To demonstrate that the Earth is a magnet, Gilbert made a sphere from lodestone and placed iron needles on its surface. The needles pointed north and dipped, following the lines of force of a bar magnet, as do compass needles on Earth

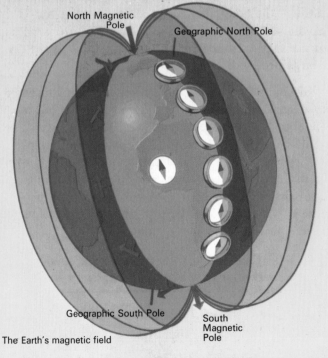

North Magnetic Pole

Geographic North Pole

Geographic South Pole

South Magnetic Pole

The Earth's magnetic field

Early ideas about electricity

The experiments in the 17th and 18th centuries were mostly with *static* electricity. A crude machine turned a ball of sulphur (or glass) which was rubbed by hand, or by a piece of leather, to produce an electric charge. In 1729 Stephen Gray and Granvil Wheeler succeeded in passing electricity along 98 yards (89·6 metres) of thread suspended by silk. They discovered that certain materials are good conductors of electricity while others are not.

The experiment illustrated (Fig. 2) shows an electrical charge being generated on a glass sphere by friction with the hands, then passing along the metal pipe, through the body of a man and along the sword. The candle, just blown out, was relit by a spark from the tip of the sword to the wire on the candlestick as the discharge occurred.

In 1746 a Dutchman connected a generating machine to a nail passed through a cork in a bottle of water. He found that the charge generated by the machine could be stored in the bottle. The experiment took place at Leyden in Holland and the device became known as the Leyden jar, although a similar experiment was also carried out at about the same time by a parson named von Kleist. The Leyden jar is still to be found, in modified form, in some laboratories.

In 1733 Charles Du Fay produced the theory that there were two kinds of electricity – known as 'positive' and 'negative'.

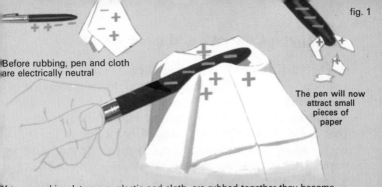

fig. 1

Before rubbing, pen and cloth are electrically neutral

The pen will now attract small pieces of paper

If two good insulators e.g. plastic and cloth, are rubbed together they become charged with static electricity. The pen in the drawing becomes negatively charged, while the cloth is positively charged

fig. 2

Volta, von Guericke and Isaac Newton

The first electric batteries developed from the discovery that an electric current could be generated by placing some damp material between two different kinds of metal. In 1800 an Italian named Volta proved that a current would flow through wires connected to each end of a column made up of alternate zinc and copper discs. Moistened pasteboard or cloth was inserted between each disc. This arrangement became known as the *Voltaic Pile* (Fig. 1). He also produced a current using a series of small containers filled with dilute acid or salt water, in which were dipped plates of zinc and copper.

During the 17th and 18th centuries many men were investigating other things. Telescopes were improved and microscopes and thermometers were developed.

Otto von Guericke invented an air pump for creating a vacuum and carried out many experiments, including a spectacular demonstration of the magnitude of air pressure. He made two very large metal cups which fitted together at the edges. After the air had been drawn out of them by his pump, teams of horses were harnessed to pull the cups apart. So great was the air pressure on the outside that it took the combined strength of thirty horses before this was done (Fig. 2).

Isaac Newton did a considerable amount of work on the properties of light. In a famous experiment he placed a triangular glass prism in a beam of sunlight passing through a small hole in a window blind and found that the sunlight was bent, or refracted, into a band of colours ranging from violet to red, as shown in the picture opposite (Fig. 3).

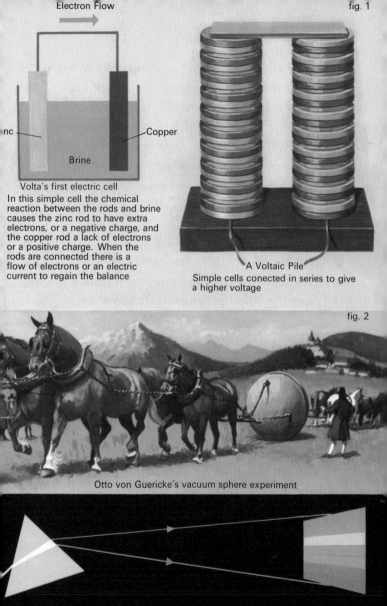

nc — Copper

Brine

Volta's first electric cell

In this simple cell the chemical reaction between the rods and brine causes the zinc rod to have extra electrons, or a negative charge, and the copper rod a lack of electrons or a positive charge. When the rods are connected there is a flow of electrons or an electric current to regain the balance

A Voltaic Pile

Simple cells conected in series to give a higher voltage

fig. 2

Otto von Guericke's vacuum sphere experiment

Newton discovered that a prism splits light into its component colours
fig. 3

New medical discoveries

As we know from Book 1, scientists and philosophers had studied the human body and its functions from very early times. Unfortunately, many of the ideas and theories, correct and incorrect, were accepted without question for a great number of years. But by the 16th century, knowledge gained through chemical experiments was beginning to make some men think more deeply about how the human body works.

A most important medical discovery was made by William Harvey in 1628. He found out that the blood is circulated round the body in one direction only by the pumping action of the heart. It had previously been incorrectly thought that the blood moved with a backward and forward motion.

Early in the 17th century a new instrument came into use that was to open up a whole new area in the study of medical and scientific matters. This was the microscope.

The first instruments were not very efficient. They were able to magnify only a very small part of the object and this was always surrounded by rings of coloured light. Nevertheless a great step forward had been taken which was of vital importance for future research and development.

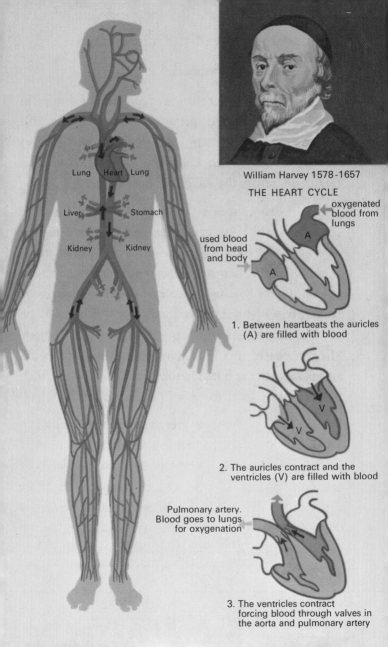

Lung Heart Lung

Liver Stomach

Kidney Kidney

William Harvey 1578-1657

THE HEART CYCLE

oxygenated
blood from
lungs

used blood
from head
and body

1. Between heartbeats the auricles
   (A) are filled with blood

2. The auricles contract and the
   ventricles (V) are filled with blood

Pulmonary artery.
Blood goes to lungs
for oxygenation

3. The ventricles contract
   forcing blood through valves in
   the aorta and pulmonary artery

The development of the microscope

Hooke and van Leeuwenhoek

During the 17th century the quality of lenses in microscopes improved greatly, and the remarkable successes of researchers like Robert Hooke and Holland's Antony van Leeuwenhoek resulted in even greater interest in the use of the microscope.

Van Leeuwenhoek's microscopes each used a single lens which he had made himself. The lens was very small and the complete microscope was not much more than about one inch (2·5cm) wide and about twice as long. It was held up to the eye and the object to be examined was fixed on a small pin which could be adjusted to give the sharpest possible image of the object. Microscopes of this kind were produced which could magnify up to four hundred times, and they gave a much clearer picture than those with a double lens.

The Dutchman made a great many discoveries using his tiny instruments, including that of the existence of red corpuscles in his own blood and the discovery of the blood's capillary circulation. Perhaps his most significant 'find', in 1683, was of bacteria from scrapings taken from between the teeth. This was long before bacteria, and their disease-causing properties, were recognised by doctors.

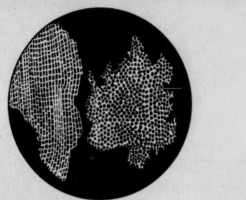

Two of Robert Hooke's drawings from his book Micrographia. On the left are sections of a cork. Hooke was the first to use the name 'cell' in describing its structure. On the right is a bee sting.

Antony van Leeuwenhoek using his microscope.

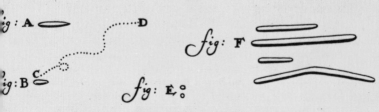

Leeuwenhoek's drawings of the bacteria from his mouth.

Gases

The advance of chemistry continued, with experiments of many kinds being carried out. Chemists became interested in respiration (breathing), combustion (burning), and the chemical changes that take place during these processes. Robert Boyle found by his experiments that a part of the air was necessary for both respiration and combustion.

Several chemists set out to discover the nature of air and other kinds of 'airs' (or gases). Four men in particular are famous for their experiments. Joseph Black discovered carbon dioxide gas which at the time (1760) he called 'fixed air'. Hydrogen was called 'inflammable air', and in 1766 Henry Cavendish discovered that water was produced when he burned hydrogen. Joseph Priestley made important discoveries about oxygen and other gases.

The fourth man was a famous French chemist named Lavoisier. He found that oxygen is present in both water and in air. He found also that hydrogen is present in water. In 1785, with another scientist, he performed one of the most spectacular experiments in the history of science. They allowed water to drip down a sloping, red-hot, iron gun-barrel. The hydrogen produced was collected in a flask and ignited by an electric spark. The liquid that was formed proved to be water.

The discovery of the various gases shows how scientific discoveries tend to be made in stages. For this reason, for example, either Lavoisier or Priestley might be said to have discovered oxygen.

When Robert Boyle pumped air out of a jar, he found that the candle would not burn and the mouse died.

Atoms

Dalton

Dalton put forward the idea that all matter is made up of a large number of atoms held together by some force of attraction. These atoms are not destroyed in a chemical reaction such as burning, but are separated and brought together again into different arrangements. Nothing is lost or gained. Dalton used these ideas to explain why the total weight of all the substances produced in a reaction is the same as the total weight of all the substances which reacted.

He also put forward the idea that the atoms of different elements have their own particular atomic weight. He used this idea to explain the relative proportions by weight in which different elements react with each other.

Dalton thought that every substance could exist in three states: solid, liquid and gas, e.g. ice, water and steam. He thought this might be because, in the solid, the atoms are stationary, whereas in the liquid and in gas they are moving about. These ideas were later developed as the kinetic theory.

Dalton's atomic theory was to have a great influence on the whole subject of chemistry, as we shall see later in the book.

Dalton's symbols for elements and compounds.

SIMPLE

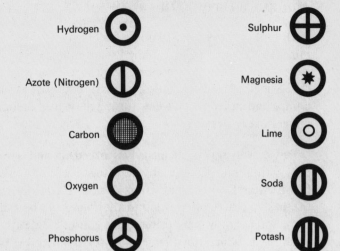

Hydrogen

Sulphur

Azote (Nitrogen)

Magnesia

Carbon

Lime

Oxygen

Soda

Phosphorus

Potash

BINARY

Steam

Ammonia

Carbonic Oxide

TERNARY

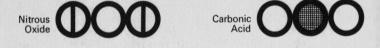

Nitrous Oxide

Carbonic Acid

QUATERNARY

Sulphuric Acid

Alcohol

Humphry Davy 1778 - 1829

Humphry Davy is best known for his invention of the miner's safety lamp. Early in the 19th century, coal mines were being sunk to depths of about six hundred feet (182·8 metres) and an explosive mixture known as fire-damp, and other gases, were causing the deaths of many miners every year.

Davy, who was a chemist, was asked to find a way of lighting mines without the danger of the naked flame of the lamp causing an explosion. He found that the best method of preventing the flame of the lamp from spreading was by using metal gauze. He designed a lamp in which the flame was surrounded by this material and thus produced the first safe miner's lamp.

Although the miner's lamp was an important invention which saved many lives, Davy's other work also had far-reaching effects. He discovered that nitrous oxide (laughing gas) not only had intoxicating properties but could also be used as an anaesthetic. He did this by breathing in the gas himself and noting the effect it had.

He was also an outstanding pioneer in *electrochemistry*. Using Volta's electric pile he discovered how to use an electric current to break down various materials into their separate elements, a process known as *electrolysis*. By this means Davy isolated potassium, sodium, barium, strontium, calcium and magnesium and helped to prove that chlorine is an element.

Sir Humphry Davy and his Safety Lamp

Oxygen can pass through the gauze
to enable the lamp to burn,
but the gauze absorbs the heat
from the flame before it can reach
any gas outside the lamp.

In 1810 Davy invented the carbon arc
lamp. He passed an electric current
through a tiny gap separating two
pieces of carbon and produced a
brilliant white light.

Here is an experiment in electrolysis you
can do yourself. Place two leads from a
battery into a glass of salty water.
A stream of bubbles will come off at
each lead, oxygen from the positive and
hydrogen from the negative. The water
is being broken down into its two
elements, oxygen and hydrogen.

Organic chemistry

The term *organic chemistry* was originally used to describe scientific work concerning substances to be found in living things such as animals and plants.

However, it was later realised that most of these substances are compounds of the element carbon, and organic chemistry now means the chemistry of the very large number of the compounds of carbon.

A raw material for many of these compounds was coal, and in the 19th century the study of the substances produced by distilling coal led to several important discoveries.

In 1856, William Perkin was experimenting with some chemicals derived from coal tar in an attempt to produce the drug quinine. Instead he produced a fine mauve dye. This was much better than the natural dyes previously used, and its discovery eventually led to the foundation of a great modern industry – the manufacture of synthetic dyes.

The study of another coal-tar product, *benzene*, enabled scientists to find out how it was made up of carbon and hydrogen atoms arranged in a circular pattern. The discovery was important because it led to the development of our enormous present day industries producing plastics, synthetic fibres, modern medicinal drugs, perfumes, insecticides and antiseptics.

Opposite: The by-products of coal.

Timber Preservative

Briquettes

Roofing

Rust Preservative

Road Tar

Aviation Fuel

Tar Fuel Oil

PITCH

Fruit Tree Spray

CREOSOTE OIL

ANTHRACINE OIL

Dyes

Rubber

M & B

Fire-lighters

NAPHTHAS

PYRIDINE

Photo-chemicals

Plastics

NAPHTHALENE

Linoleum

LIGHT OILS

PHTHALIC ANHYDRIDE

Moth-balls

Printing Inks

NAPHTHALENE OIL

Paints

XYLENE

Saccharine

Perfume

Sheep Dip

Disinfectants

Tanning

XYLENOLS

CRESOLES

TOLUENE

BENZOLE

CARBOLIC OIL

Weed-killer

niline yes

T.N.T.

Aspirin

BENZENE

PHENOL

Nylon

D.D.T.

MOTOR BENZOLE

Explosives

Adhesives

Motor Spirit

Fertilizer Sulphate of Ammonia

Sulphate of Ammonia

Household Ammonia

SULPHURIC ACID

AMMONIA LIQUOR

LIQUID AMMONIA

Car Battery

Corrugated Iron

Soap

Washing Powder

COKE

GAS

Bacteria and disease

Although the microscope had been greatly improved, little progress was made in the study of bacteria following its discovery by Leeuwenhoek in 1683.

The next big step forward came in the early 19th century. The French chemist, Louis Pasteur, the most outstanding 19th century biologist, was asked by brewers to find out why beer and wine sometimes turned sour. He discovered that the souring was caused by the presence of tiny *micro-organisms*. He came to the conclusion that these organisms were always present in the air, and proved it by many experiments. He used various flasks and found that the contents of the sealed flasks were not affected by the germs. By heating the infected liquids for a certain length of time, he killed the airborne bacteria. This later led to the '*pasteurisation*' of milk; a process which continues today.

Pasteur next turned his attention to animal diseases, particularly of sheep and poultry. He was able to show that many of these were due to bacteria which were carried from one animal to another through the air. He believed that many human diseases could be passed from one person to another in the same way, a belief that was later to be proved correct.

Pasteur's experiments led to a new science – the science of bacteriology.

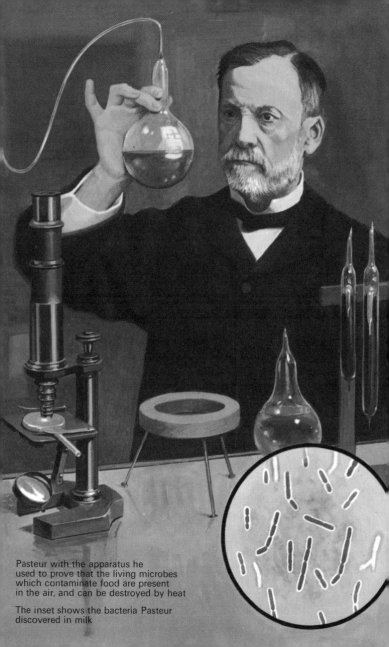

Pasteur with the apparatus he
used to prove that the living microbes
which contaminate food are present
in the air, and can be destroyed by heat

The inset shows the bacteria Pasteur
discovered in milk

The fight against infection

In 1796, Dr. Edward Jenner inoculated a boy against the dreaded disease of smallpox which killed many thousands of people. He used a *vaccine* made from the cow-pox sores of a milkmaid. The boy caught the lesser disease of cow-pox and recovered but, when later inoculated with smallpox itself, he showed no signs of catching it. The practice of vaccination, as it came to be called, was quickly adopted throughout the western world. By 1801 at least one hundred thousand persons had been vaccinated in England.

When Pasteur carried out his researches on disease-causing bacteria, he decided to adopt Jenner's idea of using a less deadly substance to vaccinate against a more dangerous disease. He found that some bacteria became inactive when cultivated outside the body, and he was able to produce vaccines from the inactive bacteria of a disease.

In the early 19th century many people were dying in hospitals from unknown causes when they should have recovered. Even minor operations proved fatal because the wounds became infected.

It was only after Pasteur had discovered that micro-organisms could be airborne, and proved that they caused infection, that hospitals and operating theatres were made cleaner. The man responsible for the greatest improvements in hospital conditions was a famous surgeon of the time, Joseph Lister. He invented a carbolic acid spray which was used in the operating theatre to kill bacteria in the air.

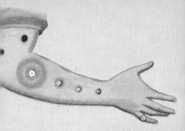

A contemporary drawing of the arm of a milkmaid suffering from cow-pox

Jenner vaccinating a child against smallpox

Anthrax bacillus and two sorts of bacteria which Pasteur found to be the cause of diseases in man. (Staphylococci and streptococci)

Joseph Lister and his carbolic acid spray

Heat and the steam engine

The nature of heat was something that baffled scientists until the early part of the 18th century. Joseph Black was the first man to realise that the quantity of heat retained in a substance was different from its temperature.

Black developed the idea of *specific heat*, by which he meant the amount of heat required to raise the temperature of a substance compared with the heat required to raise the temperature of the same mass of water by the same number of degrees.

He invented the term *latent heat* to describe the amount of heat needed to change a certain mass of a substance from one state to another, e.g. from water to steam.

The results of Black's work became very important in engineering. Using the new ideas on specific and latent heat, James Watt was able to build a steam engine which was a great improvement on an earlier pumping engine invented by Thomas Newcomen. Watt's was the first steam engine using a separate condenser.

Although employed only in mining operations for several years, by 1785 it was also being used to drive machinery in a cotton factory.

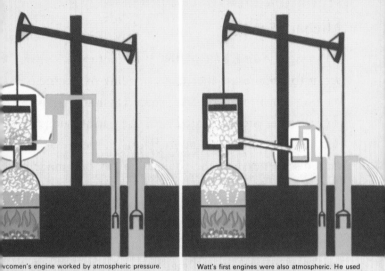

vcomen's engine worked by atmospheric pressure. weights in the water-pumps raised the piston and cylinder filled with steam. Cold water condensed steam, creating a vacuum which caused the piston e forced down by atmospheric pressure

Watt's first engines were also atmospheric. He used a separate condenser to avoid loss of heat in the cylinder, thus saving fuel and increasing efficiency

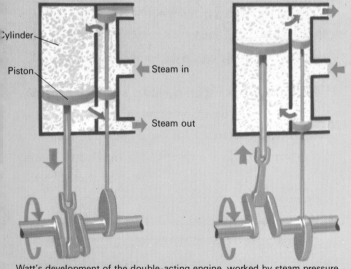

Cylinder

Piston

Steam in

Steam out

Watt's development of the double-acting engine, worked by steam pressure and conversion to rotary motion, prepared the way for steam locomotion

Michael Faraday

During the first half of the 19th century scientists began to acquire a better understanding of electricity. We owe much to people like Volta, Ohm and Ampère whose names are associated with the various units of electrical measurement, and to Michael Faraday whose later discoveries laid the foundation for our modern electrical industry.

Faraday was one of the world's greatest experimenters and he set himself the task of finding out more about light, heat, electricity and magnetism. He had the idea that if electricity flowing through a wire could create a magnetic field around it (a fact discovered by Ampère) then the field around a magnet might be used to produce electricity. His experiments with two magnets, an iron core and a coil of wire proved his idea to be correct.

From these early experiments in *electro-magnetism*, came eventually the development of the electric generator which produces electricity for our homes and factories. They also resulted in the invention of the electric motor to drive machinery and provide power for electric trams and trains. The electric telegraph, the telephone and many electrical appliances owe their development to the original work of Michael Faraday.

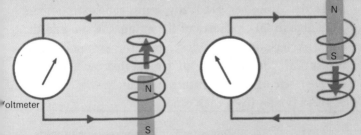

Faraday showed that when a magnet is passed into a coil, an electric current is induced to flow in the coil. When the magnet is moved back the current flows in the opposite direction. A stationary magnet induces no current

The beginning of scientific photography

Most of us may think of photography as a way of taking pictures of our friends and recording scenes and events we come across whilst on holiday. Photography has, of course, a more serious purpose in commercial life, in industry and in science.

Silver compounds which became blackened by sunlight were known in the 18th century. Later, Humphry Davy and Thomas Wedgwood made the first vague pictures by placing various objects onto material that was sensitive to light. In 1839 a Frenchman, Louis Daguerre, invented a method by which pictures could be made on silver-plated copper sheets. These pictures became known as *daguerreotypes*. In England, Fox Talbot found a way of taking pictures on light-sensitive paper and making copies from the original picture. He also discovered how to take pictures using a short exposure and he invented the terms *photography*, *negative* and *positive*. A light-sensitive material that could be coated onto glass plates was next invented.

As the processes gradually improved, astronomers were able to take pictures of the moon, the sun and the stars. A technique was developed for examining and measuring the pictures under a microscope. This enabled scientists to measure accurately the distances of these bodies from each other.

Opposite: The daguerreotype process – the beginning of modern scientific photography.

Copper plate coated with silver

Iodine fumes – Bromine fumes

Copper plate

Exposed to light in camera

Developed in mercury vapour

Unaffected bromide and iodide washed away with salt solution

More efficient telescopes

The study of astronomy was greatly helped in the 19th century by the development of more powerful and efficient telescopes.

The lens telescope, or *refractor*, was vastly improved when it became possible to manufacture high-quality lenses made from flint glass. For many years this type of glass had been used for making bottles, but no-one had made it well enough for use in lenses until a Swiss glass-maker thought of stirring the material while it was in the molten state. This removed all the air bubbles and made the mixture smooth enough to be shaped into lenses.

By the late 1800s very large telescopes of this kind were being built in America. One of them, which is still the largest refractor in the world, had a lens with a diameter of forty inches (1·01 metres).

It was not possible to make a practical lens of larger size, so scientists turned their attention to *reflecting* telescopes which used mirrors instead of lenses to enlarge the image. Isaac Newton had been the first person to build a reflecting telescope but the idea was not developed for a very long time. Today there are reflecting telescopes in use with mirrors of two hundred inches (5·1 metres) or more in diameter; one of these, on Mount Palomar in California, is shown opposite*.

* *See the Ladybird book 'How it works—The Telescope and Microscope'*

Prime focus for photographs and observing faint stars

Observation of bright stars

Mirror

Reflecting Telescope

Cathode rays and X-rays

In the 19th century a great deal of research went into the study of electricity when passed through various gases. A method was found of welding metal ends, or *electrodes*, to glass tubes. A special pump was developed for taking out most of the gas from gas-filled tubes so that what remained inside was at very low pressure. When electricity was passed through the tubes, the gas inside glowed. This interesting experiment eventually led to the development of the fluorescent light tube.

Scientists also studied the way in which the sides of the tubes could be made to glow when more gas was pumped out. The effect seemed to be due to some sort of invisible rays coming from a negative electrode, or *cathode*, of the tube. These rays became known as cathode rays. (A cathode ray tube is used in television sets.)

In 1895 a German named Röntgen discovered, during an experiment, that rays coming from a tube through which high-voltage electricity was passed, caused a chemically-coated paper nearby to glow. It was soon found that when a hand was placed in front of the apparatus, the rays passed through the flesh but left a picture of the bones on a photographic plate. Because he did not know what the rays were, Röntgen called them X-rays.

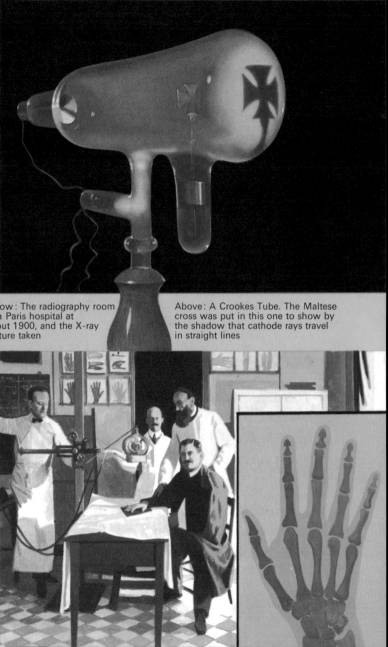

Below: The radiography room of a Paris hospital at about 1900, and the X-ray picture taken

Above: A Crookes Tube. The Maltese cross was put in this one to show by the shadow that cathode rays travel in straight lines

The theory of the atom

Pierre and Marie Curie discovered that a substance they called *radium*, obtained from a uranium ore known as pitchblende, also gave out radiation. Because of this radiation they said the substance was *radioactive*. For many years radium has been used to treat deep-seated diseases such as cancer.

Ernest Rutherford studied the rays that were emitted from the mineral uranium and found that these were of two kinds. He called them *alpha rays* and *beta rays*. He discovered that these rays were actually minute particles. Because they were constantly shooting away from their radioactive material, he concluded that the atoms of that material must be breaking up. This led to the revolutionary idea that the atom is not the smallest particle of anything but itself consists of different parts.

In 1911 Rutherford stated his theory of the atom. He said that the atom consists of a central *nucleus*, which has a positive electric charge, and around the nucleus are constantly circling *electrons* which have a negative electric charge.

The importance of Rutherford's work is immense. It forms the basis of modern nuclear physics and of the industries that have been built up to produce atomic power and nuclear energy for both war and peace.

The Curies refined tons of pitchblende to
produce a fraction of a gramme of radium

A patient receiving
modern radio-therapy

Radio waves

Following Michael Faraday's early experiments, efforts were made to find a mathematical explanation for electro-magnetism and the 'lines of force' surrounding a magnet – what we call the *magnetic field*. The work was begun by a man named Kelvin and continued by Maxwell, who foretold the possibility of radio waves.

Some years later, one of the most important experiments in the history of radio took place. A German, Heinrich Hertz, caused a spark to flash across a spark-gap at the top of a Leyden jar on the other side of the room*. It was the result of a radio wave crossing the room at a speed of 186,000 miles a second.

In 1897 another major discovery was claimed, this time by the young Italian Marconi. By using an aerial and an earth with his apparatus he increased the range of radio transmissions to a distance of several miles. During the next few years he made many further tests and sent his radio signals over greater distances. At last, in 1901, a message was transmitted from Cornwall to Newfoundland. Marconi had bridged the Atlantic by radio.

* See the Ladybird book 'The Story of Radio'

...rtz demonstrated that an electric spark jumping the gap between two spheres ...duced waves which made a spark jump between spheres on the other side of the room

Radio astronomy

By using giant radio telescopes, like the famous one at Jodrell Bank, modern astronomers are able to detect the radio waves coming from some stars. These *radio stars*, as they are called, are vast distances out in space, most of them much further away than the stars we can see. It is estimated that some are about a thousand million light years away – that is about 2,000,000,000, 000,000,000,000 miles!

The faint radio signals coming from them are collected by the big dish of the radio telescope, focussed onto the aerial in the centre, fed into very sensitive amplifiers and passed to a pen which traces out the signals as the telescope scans the sky.

Radio telescopes were developed from the radar equipment which was used to detect enemy aircraft approaching the shores of Britain during the Second World War. In fact, the telescopes themselves can be used as giant radar sets to send signals out. These signals 'bounce' off the object – artificial satellites, the sun, moon and the nearer planets – and are picked up again on their return. The first Russian Sputniks were tracked in this way, and a similar system is used to contact the communications satellites that now continually encircle the earth.

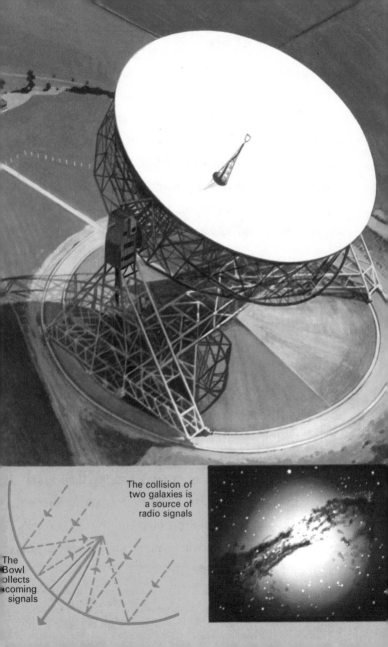

The collision of
two galaxies is
a source of
radio signals

The
Bowl
collects
incoming
signals

The secrets of life

Just as the radio telescope has enabled Man to look into the vastnesses of space, so the development of the microscope has enabled him to study the tiniest particles of living matter. The optical microscope, like the optical telescope, has a limited use; the electron microscope, which can magnify up to 1,500,000 times, is making it possible to explore things as small as living cells and viruses.

Scientists today can watch the growing, rearranging and dividing of the minute, throbbing, pulsating speck of matter that is the living cell. They can see how a single cell can multiply and develop. They can look deep into the heart of the cell and see its nucleus.

At first, the study of the secrets of life was undertaken in the pure search for knowledge. Now, scientists are seeking to find a way of controlling the multiplication of diseased cells in cancer. They are using their knowledge to transplant organs from one person to another and hope to combat the problem of one set of cells rejecting the other. A whole range of new ideas and possibilities is developing.

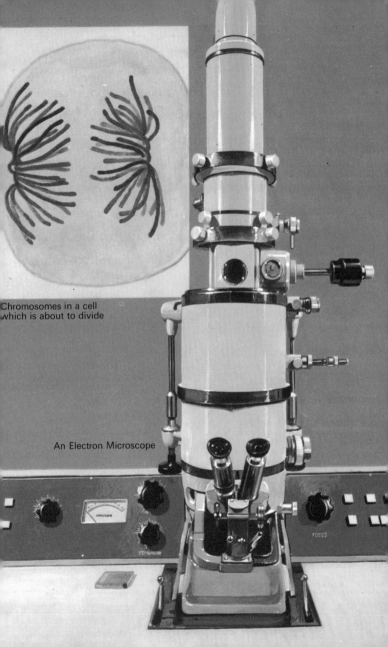

Chromosomes in a cell
which is about to divide

An Electron Microscope

Science and engineering

Science has given the world many wonderful inventions. The internal combustion engine, gas turbine and rocket motor, electric and nuclear power, the fuel cells, radio, television, complex machines and instruments of all kinds; the list is almost endless. We take everything for granted, yet almost every development has been the result of theories and counter theories and of painstaking experiments. Sometimes, but not often, something worthwhile has been produced unexpectedly by sheer good luck.

Scientific research is being speeded up even more by the use of one of Man's more recent inventions – the computer. For example, in a few seconds a computer can solve mathematical problems that would take a team of men several months.

Another remarkable machine – the 'atom smasher'– helps scientists to learn more about the exact nature and power of the atom nucleus. These giant machines (synchrotrons) hurl atomic particles at a target at a speed approaching that of light (186,000 miles a second).

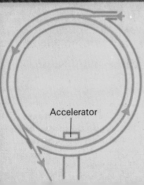

Accelerator

In the synchrotron protons are accelerated inside a hollow tube. The tube is surrounded by electromagnets which keep the protons in circular orbit. The protons are accelerated at each revolution, and make several million revolutions per second, until they are travelling at almost the speed of light

Above is an aerial view of the European Research Laboratory at Geneva. The circular mound covers the tube of the machine and has a radius of 328ft. (99.9m). The magnets contain 3,400 tons (3 454.56t) of iron and the voltage approaches 28,000,000,000

Feeding the world

For thousands of years Man has been cultivating the earth for food. As populations have increased the task has become more difficult. Three people die every two seconds of the day but three babies are born somewhere in the world every second. There are as many as fifty million new mouths to feed every year. If everyone is to have enough to eat, science must increase the food-growing areas of the world and improve the yield of the earth itself.

In Israel and other desert countries of the Middle East, work has already begun on turning the sands into soil. Dams and waterworks have been provided to improve irrigation. In areas where the growing season is short, quick-growing wheat and vegetables are being developed. Chemical fertilizers help to renew the fertility of the soil and allow more food to be grown. Scientists are even making tasty synthetic 'meat' from beans! The sea is a source of food, other than fish, that has yet to be fully explored.

In the future, science will have to play an even greater part in food production if the increasing population is to be adequately fed.

Opposite: (Top) Spreading fertilizer, killing pests and weeds and even sowing seeds can now be done by helicopter.

Series 601